Kumbh Mela

Dearest Angad,

I hope you enjoyed the Mela like "Heaven". And Happy Biday for the 25th!

♡ always
Devika.

© Rupa Classic India Series 2001

First Published 2001 by Rupa & Co.
7/16 Ansari Road, Daryaganj,
New Delhi 110 002

Set in Times 9.6 pts.

Scanning in India at
The Casa Documentation Centre.

Printed in India by Gopsons Papers Ltd.
Noida, (UP)

ISBN 81-7167-504-2

Design: Supriya Sharma

Naga sadhus stride together on their way to the Mauni Amavas bath. These sadhus have the privilege of taking the first holy dip of the Kumbh

Kumbh Mela

Text and photographs by
Ashim Ghosh

Rupa & Co

INTRODUCTION

T *he origins of the Kumbh Mela are rooted in mythology. The legend, mentioned in the Vedas and Puranas is set thousands of years ago. The Surs (Gods) needed to avenge their humiliation and defeat at the hands of the Asurs (Demons). They petitioned Lord Vishnu, the sustainer of the Universe, to help them find a solution. Vishnu's advise was for them to procure the nectar of immortality (amrit) by churning it from the bottom of the milky ocean. The Surs could not achieve this task on their own and after several unsuccessful attempts had to make an alliance with the Asurs with whom they agreed to share the nectar.*

The task at hand was a famous event in Hindu mythology – Samudra Manthan – where the Gods and the Demons actually collaborated for common gain. Of course this required extraordinary implements and a huge effort. The Himalayan mountain Mandara was considered mighty enough to be the designated churn. The huge underwater snake Vasuki was coiled around the churn, head held by the Asurs and the tail by the Surs. Then commenced a massive churning during the exertions of which Vasuki vomited huge quantities of poison. Lord Shiva came to the rescue by drinking this poison and holding it in his throat. He turned blue and this is why he

4

is referred to as Neelkanth (blue-throated). Finally, the milky ocean yielded many magical gifts, held today in great reverence by Hindus. These were a holy cow, a flying horse, Lakshmi (the goddess of wealth) and Vishvakarma (the divine architect). Right at the end emerged Dhanavantri, the divine healer and physician bearing the pot of amrit.

At this juncture the Gods, in panic at the thought of the Demons becoming immortal, grabbed the pot of amrit *from Dhanavantri and tried to flee. The ensuing battle lasted twelve cosmic days (equivalent to twelve years in our time) during which Lord Vishnu once again came to the assistance of the Gods and cut off the head of the serpent the* Asurs *were holding. The Gods thus hung on to the pot of* amrit. *However, during this war of good and evil, some drops of the* amrit *fell on four places on earth, sanctifying them forever. This is why the Kumbh – which means pot or pitcher – Mela is held in these four locations, in divisions of a twelve-year cycle. And the notion of a holy bath, or Maghisnan (bath in the month of Magh/ January) at the Kumbh is associated with the consumption of* amrit *or the nectar of immortality.*

Each of these locations is on the banks of an important river – Haridwar on the Ganga, Ujjain on the Sipra, Nasik on the Godavari and Prayag (later named Allahabad) at the triveni sangam *or confluence of the Ganga, Yamuna and the mythical Saraswati.*

One of the earliest references to the Kumbh rituals is in the Atharvaveda, *where it is mentioned that Brahma was the originator of the tradition, created to liberate and cleanse the human soul. Some experts have pegged the origins of the Kumbh in Neolithic times. The famous Chinese traveller Hiuen-Tsang, who traversed India between 629 and 645 AD stayed at Prayag during the reign of King Harshavardhana (606-645 AD). His records describe an "ageless" bathing tradition at the rivers' confluence in 634 AD, attended by hordes of people, including royalty and ascetics. King Harshavardhana is supposed to have distributed alms to the needy on the occasion.*

In the 8th century AD, Sri Adi Shankaracharya, the renowned Brahmin leader, tried to organise the Hindu religion by setting up places of pilgrimage in the four corners of India. With his well-known charisma, he propelled important priests and sadhus to congregate at the Kumbh Melas. This was to be a forum where perspectives on Hindu doctrine could be discussed, ideas exchanged, and directives, policies and reforms formulated. Other than the cleansing bath ritual of the Kumbh Mela, over the years this growing grand assembly of ascetics and priests has become an additional attraction for pilgrims.

According to prominent Indologists, Prayag is one of the most ancient cities of India. The Ashokan Pillar found here dates back to 232 BC. Prayag saw the passage of many important kings and dynasties. King Ashoka, King Samudra Gupta and King Harshavardhana all left signs of their presence in this age-old place. Centuries later, in 1583, the Mughal Emperor Akbar built a small fort overlooking the sangam *and the following year, changed the name of Prayag to Allahabad.*

In days of yore, attending the Kumbh Mela must have been a once-in-a-lifetime event, entailing considerable preparation, arduous journeys, danger from dacoits and robbers, stampedes and serious health risks including cholera epidemics. Mark Twain who visited the Mahakumbh Mela in 1895, marvelled at the "unwavering faith" of the pilgrims who "plodded for months in heat to get here, worn, poor and hungry." Sidney Low, who visited the Kumbh during the tour of the Prince and Princess of Wales in 1906, found the experience "more impressive, picturesque and significant" than anything that could be witnessed in India.

Through centuries of evolution, the Kumbh Mela has grown in scale and dimension. Today it is a vibrant kaleidoscope of perspectives on the Hindu socio-religious canvas, a combination of physical and metaphysical, real and mystical, earthly and cosmic. During the event hundreds of akharas *(sadhu sects) join the processions, gatherings and prayers. Amongst the sadhus, the Nagas (the unclothed) are the most revered. These sadhus live*

7

in the most bare conditions from caves to jungles, existing on herbs, roots and plants. The Naga sadhus of the most important akharas *have the honour of taking the first holy dip of the Kumbh. This is the signal for all the pilgrims to proceed. The holy dip at Allahabad is considered the most auspicious. It is a major reaffirmation of faith. The Kumbh is also supposed to have an impact ranging from global peace to agrarian fertility.*

The choice of locations, dates and times dictating the Kumbh Melas are specific, and pre-determined by precise astrological calculations prescribed in the Hindu almanac. The planetary alignment on those specific dates, times and locations is believed to generate great cosmic power. For the first Mahakumbh of the millenium (January - February 2001) the planetary alignment is very special and will apparently be repeated only after 144 years.

For the entire duration of the Mahakumbh several million pilgrims live in tents and ashrams, existing for days on end in stringent and basic conditions, eating simple vegetarian food and taking daily baths at the sangam. *This highly esteemed austere penance is called* kalpvas *and the pilgrims practising it are called* kalpvasis. *Thousands of canvas tents set in parallel lines is one of the hallmarks of the Mela. Pontoon bridges criss-cross the Ganga. Massive camps and kitchens cater to the teeming millions, and a huge administrative effort facilitates the smooth functioning of this mammoth fair.*

The action starts before sunrise. Winter infuses a light mist on the whole area. Slowly, religious songs, chants, conches and bells awake the sleeping pilgrims. There is always a rush for the morning bath after ablutions, and by sunrise, the banks of the river are crowded with the devout. Groups of pilgrims take turns to bathe, while one or the other keeps an eye on belongings. Some can be seen awkwardly changing into dry clothes, tolerating the mass of jostling humanity. As usually happens after a bath, there is a rush for breakfast. The Kumbh Mela offers an incredible infrastructure to host and feed millions. All the akharas *offer mass-feeding facilities, many of which are* gratis. *The landscape is dotted with tea stalls, which in the cold of January, is a welcome sight.*

Through the day one can participate in lectures, discussions, prayer gatherings and rituals. These are held in the ashrams, akharas *and temples which put up temporary structures and auditoria, resplendent with massive gates, colourful flags, idols and religious symbols. The sadhus have their own gatherings, sitting around the traditional* dhuni *(wood embers) in their unique splendour. There is an heirarchy here, with the more important sadhus being less accessible to the public.*

If it happens to be Mauni Amavas – the most important bathing date – the entire scene changes. The focus shifts to the magnificent processions and pageants.

9

Everyone rises early to find a good viewing spot. It all starts before sunrise, with millions of onlookers lining the procession paths. Those revered naked ascetics, the Naga sadhus run in hordes towards the sangam *at the prescribed time, shouting "Har har Mahadev" and "Har har Ganga" in unison. The amount of energy in the air is amazing. Through the day follow unending processions, presenting many different sects and branches of Hindu belief. The religious leader of each sect is presented to the public in splendid robes and under ornate umbrellas, in impressive gold and silver chariots, on horses, camels and elephants.*

Unimaginable shades of yellow, saffron, red and crimson paint the fiesta. Groups shuffle past singing hymns, accompanied by bands of musicians. Flags, swords, staffs and braided hair are brandished aggressively in a show of skill and strength. Occasional groups of sadhavis (women ascetics) walk past in a saffron procession. Pealing bells, Vedic chants, mantras, drums, incense and fragrant flowers permeate the atmosphere. Some sadhus do not like being photographed, and are quite capable of snatching cameras and throwing them away.

Once the sadhus have taken the first dip, it is the pilgrims' turn to cleanse their souls. The river bank stretches with human heads for as far as the eye can see. It is an overwhelming sight. Prayers and rituals carry on the entire day, into the evening. Sundown is always marked by temple bells and conches, aartis *(prayers) and* bhajans *(hymns). Ritual lamps are lit and special prayers offered.*

As coloured lights and electric installations are switched on it all takes on a slightly technological feel. The towering structures of the akharas *shine bright in the darkness, as the pilgrims and tourists walk about further feasting their senses on the evening spectacle.*

A month later those huge tents, gates, make-shift temples and towers slowly come down. Tourists, photographers, TV crews and journalists are satiated by then with the extraordinary cultural experience. The kalpvasis *are cleansed, healthy and assured of their place in heaven and the mass exodus begins, leaving behind vast empty tracts of white sand on the river banks.*

Sikh pilgrims at the sangam

Important bathing dates for the Mahakumbh Mela in Allahabad, 2001

9 January   *Paush Purnima* – full moon in the month of Paush

14th January   *Makar Sankranti* – the Sun enters Capricorn

24th January   *Mauni Amavas* – new moon in the month of Magh, the most important bathing day. Jupiter is in Aries and the Sun, the Moon and Venus are in Capricorn. A most auspicious alignment

29th January   *Vasant Panchami* – the fifth day after the new moon

8th February   *Magh Purnima* – full moon in the month of Magh

21 February   *Mahashivratri* – the marriage night of Lord Shiva and Parvati

Astrology and Astronomy

The Kumbh Mela is held every three years by rotation at four places. These are determined by certain planetary configurations and with reference to the Hindu almanac.

Allahabad : latitude 25"42'N; longitude 81"50'E
Haridwar : latitude 29"56'N; longitude 78"11'E
Ujjain : latitude 23"10'N; longitude 75"41'E
Nasik : latitude 20'N; longitude 74'E

At Allahabad the Kumbh is always held in the months of Paush and Magh (January-February) when Jupiter is in Aries and both the Sun and the Moon are in Capricorn.

At Haridwar, the Kumbh is held in Phalgun and Chaitra (February-March) when the Sun passes to Aries and Jupiter is in Aquarius.

The Kumbh in Ujjain is fixed for the month of Vaishakh (April-May) when these planets are in Libra.

At Nasik the Kumbh takes place in Shravan (July-August) when the three planets are in Cancer.

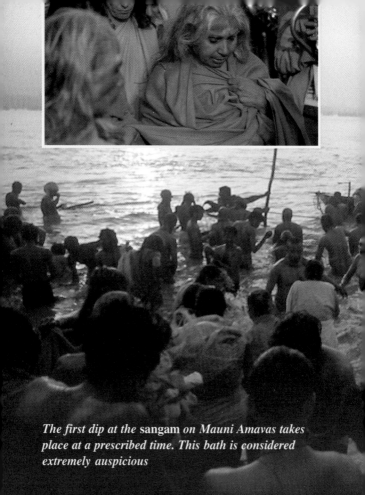

The first dip at the sangam on Mauni Amavas takes place at a prescribed time. This bath is considered extremely auspicious

Sadhavis make a powerful impact at the Mela despite their relatively small numbers

Children dressed up as Rama and Sita, staging the religious spectacle

A view of history from the triveni sangam. *The fort was built by the Mughal Emperor Akbar in 1583*

Crowds stretching to receive flowers strewn by the priests in procession

An ash-covered sadhu sits pensively in his corner. The brass pot is the karmandal, *an age-old vessel associated with sadhus*

*A Naga sadhu sets up his
installation for onlookers.
Lying on a bed of thorns
he reinforces the aura of
awe surrounding the
Nagas*

*Tonsured followers of the Shri Swami Vishnu Devanand
Saraswati sect sprint to the* sangam, *chorusing "Har
har Ganga"*

*In Hindu pilgrimages shaving the head
is a common sacrifice*

*Gearing up for the bathing ritual on Mauni Amavas.
The pilgrims are undeterred by the January cold*

The Kumbh offers the rare sight of a huge collection of religious leaders. They are presented to the public with much fanfare, under brocaded umbrellas, in impressive gold and silver chariots

*Tented colony set up by
the Kumbh Mela
administration. Several
hundred thousand such
tents provide basic
accommodation for
pilgrims on a low budget*

Pilgrims drying their sarees in the river breeze

Police are stationed at critical spots to help avoid mishaps and to render assistance to the pilgrims

In keeping with tradition, sadhus stage themselves for the benefit of onlookers during the processions

*Pilgrims camping in tents. Sarees dry in the foreground,
while groups of people occupy themselves in diverse
activities ranging from cooking to religious discourse*

*Followers proudly parade their gurus in ornate chariots
accompanied by bands of musicians*

Fairy lights outline the many make-shift structures against a darkening sky

Millions of pilgrims reaffirm their belief in the power of the holy bath at the sangam

Pontoon bridges criss-cross the rivers to accommodate the mind-boggling traffic

A procession of sadhus. Ash from the dhuni, *or wood embers, is considered sacred. It is used to bathe with as well as for ornamentation*

Sometimes during a procession sadhus brandish swords and staffs aggressively in a show of skill and strength

Matted dreadlocks are an age-old symbol of sadhus

Overview of a typical scene at the Kumbh. Well planned walkways are conducive to the comfort and control of the mass of humanity

A Pandit reading the scriptures, surrounded by his occupational materials. Thousands of priests are available at the Kumbh for all kinds of consultation and ritual ranging from Astrology to Hindu rites

A good number of elderly people visit the Kumbh in hope of salvation in their last years

*The Shiv Dwar —
one of the many
gates that mark
the entrance to an
ashram or* akhara
camp

*Far right: It is
believed that the
River Ganga
flowed out of Lord
Shiva's* jata *(hair).
The statue
presents him as an
ascetic atop
Mount Kailash
(his legendary
abode) with his*
trishul *(trident) in
hand*

Pilgrims arrive in ongoing hordes, sometimes plodding for miles to get here

Pilgrims take a breather near the fort walls

Ritual dip silhouetted in the early morning sun

Naga sadhus in procession

Women perform the ritual of tying the mauli *(sacred red thread) around a tree, with offerings of fruit and other prescribed items*

Havan – *ritual offerings
and incantation around
a wood fire*

*Far left: In the evenings
the colourful gates
adorned with religious
symbols glow against
tungsten lamps*

Roadside vendor of sindur – *thumbed onto the forehead by priests and ascetics as a sign of blessing*